The Theory and Function of Mangoes

The Theory and Function of Mangoes

Albuquerque
8/29/05

George Kalamaras

For Phyllis,

With great joy in your
light and warm face. Thank
you for your immense kindness.

George
3°

FOUR WAY BOOKS
Marshfield

Editorial Office
Four Way Books
P.O. Box 607
Marshfield, MA 02050
www.gypsyfish.com/fourway

Library of Congress
Catalog Card Number: 99-71365
1-884800-29-7

Front Cover Photo: Sadhus, householder yogi, and young boy
preparing a feast for the poor, Calcutta, 1916
(Paramahansa Yogananda on far left).
Photo by David LaBriere of the original from the collection
of Devi and Hassi Mukherjee.

Book Design: Henry Israeli

This book is manufactured in the United States of America
and printed on acid-free paper.

Four Way Books is a division of Friends of Writers, Inc., a
Vermont-based not-for-profit-organization. We are grateful
for the assistance we receive from individual donors and
private foundations.

For Mary Ann
who made — and makes — the journey with me

And for the great yogis of modern and ancient India
who have explored the realms of meditation for centuries
with ceaseless depth, love, and compassion

ACKNOWLEDGMENTS

I want to thank the editors of the following magazines in which some of these poems first appeared:

Another Chicago Magazine: "Photograph: A History of Maps" and "Bone Crushing Bone Is Not an Excuse for Love"

The Bloomsbury Review: "At Raj Ghat"

Boulevard: "If on the Train to Bombay"

Chariton Review: "Dawn Boat Ride on the Ganges" and "On the Mula River Bridge"

Cincinnati Poetry Review: "Sister and the Boy"

Confrontation: "Harmonium"

Epoch: "Usha Vishnu Bharmal" and "A Theory of Leprosy, a Theory of Tongues"

The Iowa Review: "Hysteresis"

Laurel Review: "Eating Lunch in the Old British Cantonment in Banaras"

Luna: "The Fear of Celery"

Manhattan Review: "Colligation at Harishchandra Ghat"

Mānoa: "Introrse" and "Elutriation"

New Letters: "Mud"

Puerto del Sol: "The Theory and Function of Mangoes"

Quarterly West: "A Theory of the Borders Between States"

Southern Humanities Review: "Under Water"

Spoon River Poetry Review: "A Theory of Astronomy as Inscribed in the Book of Blood," "The Black Bowl," "Buying Silk," and "Cygnus and Olor"

William and Mary Review: "Preparing To Leave"

I want to thank the following for also including some of the preceding poems in their pages:

The Best American Poetry 1997: "Mud"

The Citadel (India): "On the Mula River Bridge"

Learning English (Maharashtra State Bureau of Education; Pune, India): "Sister and the Boy"

I am grateful to the Fulbright Foreign Scholarship Board, the Indo-U.S. Subcommission on Education and Culture, and the American Institute of Indian Studies, whose generous assistance of an Indo-U.S. Advanced Research Fellowship made my months in India possible, as did a supplementary grant from the Office of International Programs, Indiana University.

For years of love and encouragement, I want to thank my parents and family. This book owes more than I can say to friends and cohorts Phil Appleman, John Bradley, Don Byrd, Forrest Gander, Ray Gonzalez, Jim Grabill, Jay Griswold, Judy Johnson, Roger Mitchell, Mark Nowak, Chad Odefey, Arthur Sze, Bill Tremblay, and Phil Woods for their years of friendship, suggestions, and poetic inspiration. Much gratitude to Devi and Hassi Mukherjee, Catherine Van Houten, and David LaBriere for the front cover photo. I am also forever grateful to my wife, Mary Ann Cain, for her love and support, always-insightful comments, and the inspiration of her own writing.

CONTENTS

I
The Theory and Function of Mangoes

II
Every Sound Is Supposed to Speak

III
A Theory of Tongues

The secret of immortality is to be found
in purification of the heart, in meditation,
in realization of the identity of the Self
within and Brahman without.

—*Katha Upanishad*
(tr. Swami Prabhavananda
and Frederick Manchester)

Thus the duende *is a power and not a behaviour,*
it is a struggle and not a concept.
I have heard an old guitarist master say:
"The duende *is not in the throat;*
the duende *surges up from the soles of the feet."*
Which means that it is not a matter of ability,
but of real live form; of blood;
of ancient culture; of creative action.

—Federico García Lorca,
"Theory and Function of the *Duende*"
(tr. J.L. Gili)

I

The Theory and Function
of Mangoes

THE THEORY AND FUNCTION
OF MANGOES

You've always loved fruit, but now
drinking cut glass seems more logical.

It's not that you're afraid, really, or
for that matter weak. Only that you're

overly intellectual about things
like cholera. Or the composition

of music, say, at Manikarnika Ghat,
the cremation grounds on the Ganges

where strange reed instruments contract
feathers of vultures perched on temple

towers. How the skin of a mango
baked at the exact degree of sun,

fed with night soil and water-buffalo piss,
could contain a microorganism that can kill

you, here, on the other side of the earth.
You've loved the color orange for as long

as you can remember. But enough's, well,
not really quite enough, as you stare

at those innocent orange globes
on the wooden cart on Lanka at the height

of the season in Banaras and wonder how
emptiness would finally feel. You want to suck

the blood of India once and for all, die
on a Friday of dysentery, and step out of the tomb

on Sunday, just to show the folks back home
you could survive. But they'd burn

you, probably, without giving you a chance,
rake your ashes through the river-bottom

mud, and hand your wedding band back to your wife.
It's for her, you tell yourself, you're

not hungry today for fruit. But you recall
the care she takes in peeling away the thick

juicy skin with the Swiss army knife, and sucking
the core. It's your core, naked like that,

on her tongue, on the old green desk, exposed
like a word with which she's trying to come

to terms, like a moment of sexual
mathematics that can no longer account

for the simultaneity of the position
and momentum of a wave, bald

like a photon in a vacuum diagram,
like the definition of a discourse

that does not contain the theory
and function of a mango. Where in your

vocabulary, you wonder, is a count of the syllables
of *emptiness*. Of *dehydration*. Of *some-words-*

have-three-beats-but-you've-really-gotta-
watch-out-for-those-with-four. Of *O.K.,-so-maybe-*

I'm-just-afraid-to-die. It's not that you're
totally scared of the wound. You've spent

many years reading Hernández, thinking, at times,
that you actually *were* Miguel, eyeing your thirty-third

birthday with suspicion, the knives in the kitchen
drawer with increased affection. But you're past all that

now by several years, headed into your forties
like a mole struck from a tunnel, like an onion

dragged from a root cellar, tentacles of hope
lifting green limbs into light. Is it enough

to simply fantasize about mangoes, take
their roundness to bed, revolve them around

the space of your brain like voluptuous
electrons as you ease yourself to sleep,

cup them like ventricular hips? Or will their threat
of cholera force you to take precautions,

even in dream — slide their orange firmness
into gigantic condoms, imagine

that they have been touched
by no other in fourteen years, rub

their smooth blond belly-fur
without breaking the skin, kiss the stem

without tonguing the core?
You've always loved fruit, you recall,

as they crawl to you from the wooden cart,
as they beckon in front of a leper

who darts out of your periphery
into an alley filled with goat shit,

as they position themselves beneath the buzzing
of flies: permanent, firm, and magnificent

like the ruins of Rhodes. You consider, finally,
the advantages of eating something known

only by weight, by two syllables, say,
rather than three or four. Have always craved

just one wild night of slosh and juice,
of the wound left open, of even an hour

alone with the color orange. Have craved it,
for as long as you can remember.

HYSTERESIS

A tiger approaches full moonlight
in a river, drinks currents

in slow, even laps, leaps from reeds
the next afternoon, covering a deer

with the buckshot of sudden
and prolonged starlight. A boy

with hypoplasia of the left arm shakes
hands with a wandering sadhu and dreams

of orange silk that night, can hear bones
in his face snap and dress for sleep, his wrist

widen, fingers of his left hand worming
toward moonlight. A fish-seller in Agra

eats carp and has visions of a Chinese
emperor cleaning his nails, a concubine

nourished only on toothpicks
and lentils. The magnetic fields

in the hypsographer's head remain
elevated, even when he no longer examines an atlas

of the Himalayas. Can you really ever return
home? Can you board that plane in Delhi, stop

in London, and not carry back mist
on Albert Street as snow to South Bend, Indiana?

Peer out across the river. Ganga unwinds
its rich slow cobra fire for miles, muddy

brown and wide. Feel moonlight in your tongue
when you drink from a tin cup, a deer forming

a new constellation in the night sky. Hear
your limbs shift with the earth's plates

when you sleep, when you shake hands
with the dark robe of a monk

in Kentucky. Turn on a lamp,
analyze star-charts, recall lying down

in a holy man's grass hut in Banaras,
his right index finger held inside your navel

for the longest minute of your life. Map the rise
and fall of your breath at sunset

as you measure the pause in each passing
field. See a carp floating gold

over the Himalayas, darkening
wheat, following you home.

MUD

A bus driver from Delhi to Agra
says he plays tabla. Four of his fingers
are stumps, cut roughly above the knuckle.

I've got five children, he says,
and four who are no more. What happens
to our losses? Do they fly away

like the green parakeet you let escape
into towering oaks while cleaning the cage
when you were six? Do they cling

to ponds on the underside of the cup, partially
hidden but warm? A carp floats gold
through the smoky Delhi sky, the shade

of a dead pig at dawn. Something is always
covered in mud. The scent of her
voice, the plaid of that wool skirt

she wore that rainy afternoon when she asked
for forgiveness, and you sat, silent,
drawing on a cigarette. A shift in polar light

can darken Bihar, make birds brittle
as water-buffalo chips set out to dry
on sides of huts. A cold, gold leaf

on a jungle floor is not gold, is not
the floor. An astronomer lecturing
on the merits of primitive star-charts

is not the night sky in a cave but a form
of grace, body-bound but smart, caught
in the net of his mathematics. You draw

a hexagon in the mud and count
your failures. You count your fingers
to make sure. Mistakes blossom

like rare and familiar flowers, hothouse blood,
huge piles of gravel at the roadside
steaming like fresh bones from a hunt.

You want off the bus. You want to drown
yourself in the stagnant monsoon
pools of a rice field, smother in warm

water-buffalo shit, witness for yourself
a gherao, where the workers finally unite,
surround the evil landowner like a ring

of musk oxen, and threaten him
with spears of asparagus.
But all you see are those women

who carry huge gravel pans
on their heads, who report pelvic
pressure in their early thirties

from walking up and down
stone stairs balancing heavy pails
of milk, whose babies thirst for wood

and glimpse at birth the flight
of a green parakeet, the texture of oaks.
Something's always having its way

in mud, hidden in the crack in the gourd
of the sitar you bought in Banaras, stitched
in the tabla's goatskin, gripping

the steering wheel of a bus and guiding it
all the way from Delhi to Agra to Delhi,
through the heat, through starlit holes.

With the four lost souls of one's
youth. With the shade of her skirt
and scent of wet wool, even now —years later—

when you reach to touch your wife. With a tip
of asparagus freshly pulled from mud,
no longer hidden and harmless, but real.

PHOTOGRAPH: A HISTORY OF MAPS

A young girl asks you to take her
picture, breath draws itself in through your ribs

as you shift your feet in the sand and consider
the colonization of ants. One culture

cleating another into servitude
is never a euphemism. One person's sudden love

for a stranger can solidify into eutectic
plates, harden the earth and snap. The rickshaw

that brought you here is not necessarily affection
but a map marking the rickshaw wallah's death

by age forty. Statistics never lie, your
records say, especially when they pertain

to mangoes. How three mangoes
arranged on a plate in Poona resemble

a woman, a man, and something androgynous. How
they form into a goitered wishbone

lodged in the throat of a heart
patient in Des Moines, count the country

orange and add cholera to your list
of fears. But you needed the ride,

needed to sit, like you need to preserve
this young girl's face for the empty place

on your office wall back home. India *is*
the other side of the planet, your textbook

tells, yet you sense a sudden growth
in Indiana oak and maple, even here

beneath Poona palms, hear, that is, a eutrophic
lake enter your spine and engage itself

in reducing and dissolving oxygen in ways
which nourish the basalt content

in your blood. Your cells limp,
your heart limps, your nerves clear a moment

to euphonium, to the higher pitch
of wind whenever violet appears radiant

in the forehead of a slowed, persistent breath.
But you need her smile, require

how her left foot turns that way on its side
with the shyness of goldfish,

with the patience of a mantra
strung out all through the splay

of the day into japa. With the care
in unconsciously hiding dirt. You scrape

your brain to hear its rich cortextual
pulse, wish you could offer her something

real, something solid, like your hand
in marriage, or your wife, or maybe a ring

of bandits who would see her home
after the bank, or even an x ray, say,

of your lower lip, which clearly
demonstrates the saline content

of your affection. But one question always leads to
the lake. One solution is to dissolve

into the ants at your feet, bust
the borders mountains make

of space. One person's culture
for a stranger can harden into curds,

into love, into the black crusts
of usury spread like broken bread

beneath you. Into a drawing in
of breath over the history of maps,

through minnow-holes in your ribs, which,
as you stand there waiting, do nothing but snap.

THE FEAR OF CELERY

The Aghoris inhale the life-force
of the dead by drinking out of a human

skull, cover their bodies with cremation
ash, bury their sexual heat

in the left foot of Kali, pressed
like a black coconut

on the pale chest of Shiva. The Udasins
hear a radio wave in chanting the name,

Shrichandra, an earthquake in humming
leaves, and inhale deeply the burning

grass of Banaras summer, insisting
that *God is joy.* You've never before

experienced 122-degree heat nor such hunger
for raw vegetables. What you hear

in your spine is not your ponds
drying but Kali Yuga giving way

to Dwapara Yuga, a faint stirring
of hope, a possibility of soup

in the uncut onion, carrot stew
for the beets. Search the heavens

with a flashlight, the galaxies
in the sushumna with Jupiter. The afternoon

vultures that circled your apartment sleep in the moon
of someone's flesh. Feel for the chemotactic

shape of a cigar a roach makes
as it feeds its way unseen into your shoe,

for the familiar face of a stranger
you pass on narrow rickshaw-thick

lanes, for the chervil in the dish of fresh salad
you worship but cannot eat. Are you sure

this is what you wanted, you wonder, having come
this far to crave uncooked food, to sit

on a wool blanket meditating in summer silk,
feeling a scratch of moonlight that spills

Tantric heat into your bones, your life beginning over
with each creaking door, each hollow of the chopping

block, your spine introduced to the shaggy stalk
of a labor pain? Listen to the snap of celery

in the next room, the crunch of a coconut
like a human skull slicing open

the dark, warm milk boiling again
its meat in the pot, green threads giving way.

A THEORY OF ASTRONOMY AS INSCRIBED IN THE BOOK OF BLOOD

This is the road of the lost galaxy.
This is a road stolen by starlight, fur,

and damp wool. This road winds centuries together
like a comet tail braided into long black hair

and hugs the river like a second river
turned inside out into entrails

of bees that reveal walking fish,
snail-men, and stone. You wonder

what lies on the other side of your skin,
if capillaries are really capillaries

or cords of light dropping elongated bees
into electrical paths of blood. Red ochre

slabs of Durga Temple cannot compete
with the golden dome of Vishwanath

further north where Asi Road changes names
the way a man puts on a clean shirt

because it's Sunday. The way the goddess herself
shifts without notice from Parvati —

whom all the fishermen love — to Kali,
dancing on the chest of her husband

with her necklace of fifty human skulls.
Women in their Sunday saris carry away

in secret a drop of goat's blood
sacrificed on the temple floor, moan

for the Milky Way to release those too-tight
petticoats, give this sound unknowingly

to the flour, baking it into roti.
The men eat deeply of flat bread

and, when no one looks, peel
a hidden scab in their right ear, bending

to hear the migration of snow geese
in Canada, the pumping of feathers

over a deep African lake. How might
the teeth of a jaguar in Bolivia make their way

unseen into a Banaras curry? Men eat okra
and believe it's okra. Women

cook with turmeric but know
it's not just orange powder

bartered for on Asi for one or two paise.
They sense the stance of the pear

far back in their throats, the long bone
of a fish lodged there

like evening. It blossoms
in the womb at the exact moment

when a water buffalo on crowded Asi
notices a woman and gently nudges

her belly. A porridge of bees
slides white light down

from some banished star as strange heat
passes from whiskers to pink tongue

to long calm water. This is the road
of the urgent vowel. This is a road of lost

tongues, of speech between men and
women, women and fur, splayed and re-glued

like braided breath. This road winds centuries
along the river, a river with a second skin,

an animal turned inside out into constellations
of bees whose humming guides the blood.

BONE CRUSHING BONE IS
NOT AN EXCUSE FOR LOVE

*Those who die in Kashi go straight
to heaven.* The sadhu's words burn

the ossicles of your inner ear with sulfur oxide.
Soldiers at Godaulia Crossing carry shotguns

as they break for a smoke near the banks of holy Ganga.
Bone crushing bone is not an excuse for love,

can never camphor the corpse of the university
student whose death last month just outside city limits

caused campus riots, cannot replace a fallen peepal leaf
lying in a pool of saliva further north

in the city in front of Durga Temple.
Divine Mother would never be displeased

to see last night's monsoon pooling
in the face of a monkey who guards the shrine

in shrieks. What might be said has already been said.
That is all. That is all one needs

to fear. Count the seconds it takes
to lift Jupiter one time up and down

the core of sensitive spine, revolving it deep
inside, around nerve ganglia of stray

and forgotten rivers. Hold constellations
of inner peace far enough away from *left* and *right,*

yes and *no,* two centuries from your sexual heat.
Your galactic gaze becoming a widening wingspan.

Then, kiss the earth three times squarely
on its lost crane, the constant sky

in a green almond. Die, if you must,
in the city itself, in pure river-light dawn

spun from white, white eggs of a cobra
curled like liquid rope around a nest

of burning snow and cigar-fate breeze.
Do the sadhu's words cure or disturb the stirrups

of your inner ear? *To be a ghost in Kashi,*
he repeats, *is even better than having heaven at all.*

COLLIGATION AT
HARISHCHANDRA GHAT

A family of eight stands on the banks of the Ganges
tossing garlands of marigolds on the gold-sheeted corpse

of a person without a face. Vultures peer
down from towers of Harishchandra Crematorium,

dark with the soot of thousands each year
whose eyes go up in dust, whose gold glows

hot an instant, then cold, whose arms reach
charred clouds into mud-soaked rakes,

into the red pan-drenched teeth of men bent
into a constant song of scraping. Whose bodies

smoke, androgynous, like thin gray ghosts
feathering brick with the water's dark light.

This is your first ride on the river, but the pull
of its current is familiar. The texture

in its wind, a rich stippling of isolated stars
which liquefies into an indistinct constellation,

the pawing of a horse in your chest. Harishchandra
Ghat, a death harbor churning in the wake

of a haricot on your tongue. The way
your small wooden boat curves over each rising

wave is a collision of in-going
and out-going breath, a colligation

of color that eases into your thorax
like the slip of a tempered voice. You wish

your boatman wouldn't stop for you to watch,
that you could keep moving past this

weeping, grant at least this family a chance
to privately meet their river-bottom mud. You begin

to study what's there beneath you. You want to name
this wave, *Karen*, that one, *Maybe-I-shouldn't-*

have, this other, *What-good-is-there-anyway-
in-forgetting?* You want to touch her wetness

just once more beneath wool, take that cigarette
out of the mouth of memory and finally answer

her, placing it on a bed of straw beneath the tautness
of a freshly laid corpse. You want

to finally tell your father, *Enough!*,
that his leaving was a tegument of time

that clung to you like a second
skin far too long before you found a way to take it

toward dissolve. The old Brahmin priest
casts Vedic mantras over the still faceless

corpse, waves a river of incense like muffled, ignited
breath, strikes tiny cymbals in his right hand

as the slow wood beneath begins to burn. Something
in the circular motion of air disturbs you.

Is it true, you wonder, that a thin strand
of smoke at the last minute spirals out of the crown

chakra one terrible moment to look with compassion
upon the fragment of dust that took it

each day to the road crew to chop stones
in Calcutta heat, to the scraping of laundry

on Banaras river-rock? That hauled it to bed
in Bombay each night at 11:00, where starlight

in the shape of a man or woman glowed
smoke within fingers, just beyond reach

of touch or tongue? That lugged it, hungry,
to an Agra market, braving the incessant braying

of goats, the blue-black buzzing of cholera
around mangoes, just to check the firmness

of beets for soup? Something in the air
disturbs. Something in the priest's soft spell

of words invites your tongue, strengthens your cords.
Although you have not spoken, sounds

of death coat small iron disks
with mantric sense, give the dissonance

of memory shape, the distance
in shape, music. Spaces between

his words disperse, accumulate timber
from a discarded pier, wood-pilings sunk years

in your mud, driven heavily into your heart.
You want to look away, feel you are intruding,

but the boat bobs there, oddly, between waves.
Maybe-I-really-should-have. What-if-he-hadn't-

left-in-the-first-place? What-memory-is-there-
anyway-in-forgetting? You want to place burning gold

marigolds at the feet. Rub a star like broken glass
in the forehead to the north. Uncloak the face

of this woman or man who has taken you
into its still corpuscular pulse, into

its breathless bending smoke and wafting
death, into its sound of singeing

flesh. Weep with the family over wisps that finally escape
as fragments of work and touch and Tuesday-evening

soup into the deeper darkness
of brick, into a swathing of soot

that climbs out of the burning
wood, gathers in muddy-brown feathers

of huge perching birds to guard the thick
towers with such compassion, such love.

II

Every Sound Is Supposed to Speak

EATING LUNCH IN THE OLD BRITISH CANTONMENT IN BANARAS

After five weeks you hope to find food
you can eat, something American, maybe,

to firm your stools. But it's spaghetti,
"Parisian style," which in India might mean

worms. You dip your bread in the juice,
imagine the blood that has traveled telegraph

lines from Delhi to London to Delhi: the scimitars,
the pitchforks, poles of the Bengal Lancers, crushed

beets tossed like torn testicles at the walls
of Red Fort. The waiter, hobbled by your desire

for cheese, assures you that the water buffalo
that has wandered into the garden

might mean the coming of monsoon. You decide
that anything would be welcome to cut the heat,

even the high prices of the cantonment, even the water
spots on your glass that could contain a microorganism

and make you want to die. Even the fever
pitch of Bombay show tunes hung in the fan

above you slowly slurping
122-degree Banaras air. Yesterday,

out of boiled water, you told your wife,
*I don't even **like** Pepsi,* as you set out in search

of cola and a bite of sugar. She lay on the floor
of your flat, washrag over her forehead, muttering,

Be careful; the paper says 110 dead. How today
the cantonment seems like a different city: no honking,

no fumes, no beet stalls and cow droppings,
no urine smells of men against the walls.

How the British might have slit themselves silly, let
the blood into cups, kept leeches as house pets, slapped

their wives for saying, *Oh, Darling.*
To be at the summer cottage in York.

How the quiet and shade of the cantonment
might be a place to find firm shits,

good blood, and no worms. To bring a bit
of Londontown back to keep the ponies true

and the cows from poking the trash. *Grated cheese,*
you hear yourself repeat with something like disgust

or self-hate in your voice. And the waiter bows,
Yes, Baba, and brings you another fork.

THE BLACK BOWL

You hold the bowl in your hands
like secret blood. Feel yak bone,

smooth like an unformed star.
Hear the stirring of a herd

of Mogul horses push through the Jamuna River,
a night of full moonlight fire

marble in the Taj Mahal. You turn it
over, like any man or woman

looking for love, lost, perhaps, centuries
before in the unfinished scroll. Teeth

mark its base as if Kali had hold of it
in a struggle with Shiva. Like a tiger

without a swan. Like a bowl of porridge
mistaken for black rain. Remember

a murky night. Men and women slip
from sleep into icy water. See your slow face

in the dull of its shine. There are letters
at home you have not read. There is lightning,

still, in the long lines
above the city, last night's monsoon

pooling in potholes and gravel
valleys, a spark in the bowl

like the beginning of a thought
four centuries ago traveling through

your fingers. You want to hold your breath
while the world stops. Fill your body

with galactic gaze, with seeds
of possibility? With currents of eel-fire

from the ocean floor. Recall mantric sense
in the name, *Lahiri Mahasaya.* See him

seated in lotus posture in Banaras,
talking to his disciples one afternoon

of omnipresence, suddenly gasp for breath
and say, *I am drowning in the bodies of many souls*

off the coast of Japan! Hold the cable
the following morning in India. Hear syllables

of *love* and *hope* and *we'll-be-there-shortly-dear*
in the names of a number of those whose ship

had indeed sunk the day before
near Nippon. Why is it you feel uneasy

when starlight in Toledo pours through a prism,
and a child in Poona suddenly develops

dysentery? When the car refuses to start,
and you remember that you forgot

to pet the cat? When the coffee grinder sounds
like a yellow bird, and you dream of painting

the toenails of your left foot
with mustard? When you walk out

onto the lawn and find a dead sparrow
covered in motor oil? The brown of your eyes

moves through the collarbone
of a yak. Your shoulders have ached

ever since you entered the little
shop. Ever since you bent to pick up the bowl,

something in your life, you realized,
was missing. Then, feel your stomach, scooped out

like an old bark boat covered with furs.
Turn centuries through your fingers

like a sadhu counting japa on rudraksha
beads. Hear the stirring of love

begin to fade like Sanskrit, disappear
with hieroglyphics at the base

of a star pushing through the dark water
of many bodies that continue to float

through ether, that fire
marble in hooves of horses, entering

your hands with secret bones, sparks
of dark ectogenous sound

in a bowl of names, a coast
of possibility, in a bowl of black rain.

DAWN BOAT RIDE ON THE GANGES

What is the source of the Ganges?
Is it a snowslip, only, from the high Himalayas?

A distant galaxy caught white a moment
in Lord Shiva's hair, winding through

holy Hardwar? The body of a leper
bloated purple in the river

reminds you of an African violet
blooming no more than five feet

from a rock where a dhobi beats your clothes
clean. Its right arm upturned like a beggar's,

frozen by its own incessant question. To ask
a tiger to sleep on a sofa in a widow's front parlor

suggests the transfusion of starlight
for blood? You enter the sound

of a gong in your heart, bells
from an unknown river temple that come an instant,

then break out over fields. Deer scatter
like thoughts sent out in sequence

into the future to trace themselves back
to an archetypal thread. *It's easier*

for a camel to pass through, you think,
but then you wonder what goods, exactly, are hidden

in the camel's humps. What bacteria
are really Bactrian rubies disguised

as sun in frayed fur. What stars form fish there
in deeper pools of well-water grasped

in slats of a bucket. Carp come to still river
water almost out of nowhere. A photon appears

suddenly in a vacuum tube. A peepal tree
on the west bank spontaneously combusts,

then goes to ash. Someone is dying again
in Bhopal, in Banaras, in Rajasthan, killed

by the green scarf of a grenade. A corpse
is carried to the edge for river rites, burned

in front of a weeping woman and son, twelve
civilian men watching on with shouldered rifles.

Morning light enters pale wisps of almost-human smoke.
Sunday dawn, and the world begins and begins and begins.

TWO PLUS TWO

Pythagoras was certain that two plus two
only equaled four, that just birds could fly,

that three centuries later no one named
Alexander would even be born, much less

ride a white horse, and turn back mysteriously
from India only after sitting privately

with a naked sadhu for hours on a dirt road.
But a pyrometer placed in snow

at the foot of the Himalayas
can detect the slithering of a python

hundreds of miles below in Bengal,
knows that the temperature of snow

can become the pyrosis in a boy's heart.
The pull of planets is not simply

a restriction but a way of seeding
possibility. Newton's apple, a lift

of aboriginal bees when mist presses
your chest. The wall in your room

is not a chance occurrence but incarnations
of thought, centuries of deeds you performed,

gathered as wood blocks to screen you
from the dispersal in stars, fluidity

in milk. To lean against at rare moments and let you feel
human. To one day, unexpectedly, need something

more, move your hips and kiss swirls
of knotty pine, hearing your own inner sound

enlarge to silence as a way to bury
your morning oats. You step into Banaras's

Durgakund Road, barely avoid rickshaws, nudging
goats, the persistent flies that spin

blue-black starlight from tails of water buffalo,
fierce eyes of a holy man who looks into you

with centuries of recognition, with a familial lifting
of a clay pot above his head, suddenly smashing it

in your path. White, white dust
rises ghosts of bees that hum

in your right ear. This must be what learning
to walk was like, you think, finally clarifying

gravity, recalling the weight of being
one year old in your crib, testing wood slats

as you work fingers into that pearl
in your mother's mouth. The residents

of 283 Nana Peth in Poona said that trickling
sand had become a recurring feature as the wall

of their neighboring building verged
on collapse. But the two people killed

ignored warnings, moving back
into the house exactly five minutes before

it fell. You step back into the shade
of a lassi wallah's canopy. Torn burlap,

another view of heaven from the perspective
of an ant. You find the holes oddly comforting

like last week when you thought you were dying,
malarial shaking, your pulse slowing

to the pace of planets, the whole universe rotating
brilliant a moment in your spine. Recall that story

of a Tibetan lama flying in sparrow from the bottom
of a well, of Alexander refusing to tell his men

what the sadhu said, but turning them back
toward Macedonia, continually massaging

his chest, dying months later in Egypt
of pneumonia. What was he saying, you wonder,

with that smashing? The stranger next to you on the street
shakes his head, *Crazy sadhu.* But what species of bees

might be road dust? Might mist the chance
lift of a holy man's pot, swarming back

your many lives as cilia in your small intestine?
Might pollenate there from shards of clay

into a buzzing of *OM* in your right ear?
Pythagoras would calculate grains

of dust into a theorem about the sum
of the squared lengths of sides of a right triangle

equaling the square of the length of the hypotenuse,
would insist that two plus two never equals

salt, that ritual flights of lamas
were geometric tricks, that his arithmetic

could expose the pythoness at Delphi
for a fraud. But to think that a thought

traps in the tongue, thrashes in shallows,
and does not etch centuries of saliva

is to avoid the swirling grain, not hear bees split walls
into sound. But to consider Newton's apple, his test

tubes and stiff white coat—even that shock of hair—
forms of sulfuric acid caught as a moment

of math is to sift breath for spells,
each word for the pyrolytic vowel.

To worship, through burlap, frayed holes
as stars. A ripped canopy on a crowded street

as calm. The cracked pot and sadhu's eyes
before you as a melting down of human fear

into sound. A sudden lift of dust that swirls
as bees, then dissolves to air, dissolves to ground.

SISTER AND THE BOY

Like everyone else, you came
for God. Pilgrims from Tamil Nadu
in their bright saris

and baggy dhotis, wandering sadhus
with their bamboo dandas and brass
begging bowls, a few Westerners

like you dotting the street
here and there like pale shadows
of the British Raj. Even the leper

following you near the bathing ghat, pleading
with you, *Please, Sahib, please,* the open sore
in his right palm as if he had just been taken down

from the cross. Like everyone
who has come, you cut
through the chaos of scooters, goats,

and cows. And for you, the constant banter
of children practicing their English
hallo's, some sincere, some—you were warned—

just finding a new way to ask for a rupee.
But you came, like everyone, for Mother
Ganga. Centuries through this, the oldest city

on earth, she's unwound her rich slow cobra
fire into the hearts of the faithful
who travel far to bathe daily at her

banks. Centuries she's come through
the charred piles of mud and ashes
of those lucky enough to die

here and be burned at Manikarnika Ghat.
Don't worry, you had told your mother
long-distance, *it's not really that*

far—just the other side
of the planet. The hesitant step
of her, *I know,* turns now

in the uphill pace of the rickshaw wallah
whose rubber-thonged feet pedal your wife
and you through the narrow lanes

of Banaras, cutting through scores
of scooters, pilgrims, and dung. Like everyone,
you came to create God. Mold him

or her or it in the light of your own
design. Give calm to the choking dust
and smoke. To behold, just once, in the dawn

waves of Ganga the glittering scales
of a snake. To touch the unfolding
universe in her shedding sacred morning

milk. You came for Ganga. You came for God.
And yet your skin betrays you. Out of the brown
curiosity of the faithful, street vendors rummage

your eyes for a rupee, illegal money
changers ask you your way, an Indian teen
in dark glasses and slicked-back hair—

looking remarkably like an American
50's hood—offers you hash. A young girl
follows you down the street, repeating

in sing-song hopscotch rhythms, *Hallo,*
hallo, Sister and the Boy. Hallo, Sister
and the Boy. Out of the strength

of a thousand Indian suns of only
a week, you fall into yourself
like a kite folding into a fire. To hold

three days ago in Delhi a mother
and son a look away as she leaned
into your stopped cab, pointing

to her mouth, then her son, *Oh, Sahib, please,*
please —inspect her like a piece
of exotic fruit, and toss the core

to the dogs. To have the pus
of a leper this morning in Banaras
inches from your lips and refuse it

even a rupee, refuse to give it
a kiss. To hear the slip
of a girl's dawn voice following you

down narrow lanes, measuring your heart
as it echoes off the River Ganges, leaving
it for dead with her smile in the dust

and dung. Like everyone, like those
who have swarmed in a thousand Indian suns,
you came for Ganga, you came for God.

HARMONIUM

You watch a sadhu at the Kabir festival open
the mouth of God. Birds breathe in the bellows.
His mother lies on the shadowed stone

floor, one of 15,000 who seek starlight
in afternoon ashram grounds, who feed
for three days in Banaras each year

on the full moon of June. You cannot see
the harmonium but imagine reeds, the holes
opening after a long struggle, can hear planets

in your spine rearrange and lift you out
of the 122-degree heat. He cannot claim
this music as his mother but can eat out

the orange endocarp of a mango. Manage
to encode the most secret mantras of his tongue
in the enclitic notes that surround her

feeding, a hunching into curry
that can never allow the use of her
left hand. She cannot speak

the syllables of his new sacred name
without first craving saffron
rice, without again enduring the death

of her husband, Prashant. You remember
vultures circling your apartment
on Lanka when you stepped into summer

sun and realized how many miles
moonlight travels to impregnate
the electrons of an air conditioner.

He recalls the smell of a corpse
at the moment of birth and meditates daily now
at Manikarnika Ghat, one of the cremation

grounds on Ganga. She senses something different
in the taste of her soup, in peels
of carrots, in the gentle thrashing of reeds

and opening of holes, even here at the tomb
of the parents of Kabir, even here,
among thousands of other mothers.

AT RAJ GHAT

This is where Gandhiji was burned at death.
What remains is a square of black marble

and where the head might be, an urn of ash
as a memento, for the Mahatma

now swims in the Jamuna and borders
New Delhi. So many deaths and burnings

glow in votive candles and marigolds
dropped like golden dust across the slab:

Jawaharlal Nehru, Indira Gandhi,
and at the eastern end of Raj Path,

India Gate, a 42-meter-high
stone arch of triumph that bears the names

of 90,000 Indian Army soldiers
who died in World War I, the North-

West Frontier operations, and — confused —
in the 1919 Afghani War.

This is where Gandhiji's flesh burned brightly,
shooting up from beneath mounds of flowers

like a sudden brush fire, or a flare
saying, *save me, save me, save me, and you*

save yourself! Marigolds shiver in breezes
pouring back from the river and spill dust

like tiny ingots of blood that glow gold
in sun. You are one of thousands of pilgrims

who touch the stone, who bow into yourselves
and feel cool blackness below burning gold.

What remains is a slab of black marble
and a beautiful park with labeled trees

planted by Queen Elizabeth II,
Dwight D. Eisenhower, and Ho Chi Minh.

A THEORY OF THE BORDERS
BETWEEN STATES

Cup a fly in the guest lodge in Calcutta.
Hold it in your right hand and hear the earth

begin to spin then stop. Light
from the ceiling fan falls in slats,

makes your fingers opaque. But hold
a flashlight against skin and see blood

begin to burn translucent, red, magenta.
Now the fly escapes red juice

to sit upside down on a ceiling crack and contemplate
the other side of sound. You consider Devraha Baba,

the naked Vaishnava, living three hundred years,
walking the Indian subcontinent for months to dispel

dark spots on foreheads of the feral, suddenly
disappearing one day in 1990 like sacred ash

in wind. Those Babas in Banaras who perform
the fire-austerity, sitting inside a ring

of smoldering cow dung, balancing on their heads
clay bowls of burning coals, stepping in their still

perfect poise across thresholds
of death. You have crossed

the border from Bihar into West
Bengal, but what lies in between?

When you leave the summer heat
of one state for another,

can you ever hear polar ice beneath
begin to split? Mercurial light

of Mars pouring sulfites through the glandular curve
of a woman who sells fish in Calcutta? You hear

the fly buzzing like a world
that will not stop but can only see a thin line

of plaster pulling apart in lightning
curves, hear the rotation

of the fan like a record that skips.
You examine your hands

but cannot describe the sound
of burning coals in your groin

when you turn to sleep and can
only recall scent of smoldering

dung. The fingers of a woman
selling fish on the Hooghly River

Bridge in Calcutta contain starlight
for blood, secret scales that lodge in your throat

unsung mantras. You hold
the flashlight against the cup

of your hand, see blood turn
inside out, the world begin

to burn. The dark spot, in your palm,
that was the fly begin to shine.

BUYING SILK

Traveling by bicycle rickshaw
past silk shops on Madanpura

is a thirst for moonlight
that will solidify sun. Buying things

is a craving for bread, becomes a sacrament
that makes you only temporarily feel real.

Yesterday the one-armed man at Dasaswamedh Ghat
selling rudraksha beads stung you

with his best stance. Probably no more
than forty, you think, but bent and shrinking

every day. What was the cost of your fingering
each bead, each dried pit of fruit, blanching it

with lust in Banaras mist? Was it your breathing,
you wonder, that made him hunch a little more, shocked

from the press of your need?
Seeds of desire percolate

in the subtle channel of your spine where
centuries of deeds from your past lives lodge

like bent bones in the throat.
Monsoon washes nothing away

but a little heat, and in its place
the cobblestone lane becomes a blocked aorta

thickening with steam and slow rain.
In any moment of weakness, one becomes

that weakness, loses his way
in a series of discrete future

moments, in the dancer's-splits grasp
of a watch. This emptiness in your gut is not any more

empty than gazing with a telescope
through the worn shell of an ostrich egg,

stunned by the sudden absence of Saturn. Yellow light
catches the orange thread of a renunciant's

robe flapping a broken wing against a calm
of dyed cotton. But Banaras in summer is never

Calcutta. Calcutta, not even Calcutta
in the clench of monsoon mood making you

dark. Last Tuesday in Sassoon, scores of passersby
ignored the corpse of a homeless man being eaten by a dog

on a busy street as they passed the dead house
of Sassoon General Hospital. A rag picker

who stays in one of the small huts near the dead
house said that she saw him on Monday evening,

lying in the spot, writhing in pain.
Any series of moments strung out in logical sequence

might make more sense as an aneurism or a sudden orgasm,
brought on in sleep by the press of clean sheets,

backfiring through the wrong nerve channel
into a long-held desire to eat

horse. One could wear only orange,
be a wandering monk, continuously

circumambulate a nest of cold cobra
eggs, and still not learn to fly, hunched

into a thickening of flesh, into a desire
for chickpea and potato curry

as if it were your lost and future
weight, contemplating in secret dark that hushed

silver anklet above her tender curving
toes, unwound galaxies contained

in her auburn braid, the brown river moon
of her waist. One could finally spot

the shop after many wrong turns, stop
the rickshaw wallah with a slap

on the back at the precise moment
of silk, descend into a cough of dust.

Mount two stone steps into luminous shed
skin, into wheat-fields

of fabric bowing in the breeze
your persistent breath makes

as it searches for more. Take a roll
of silk in your hands with the tentative

certainty of being—for a moment—human,
the first meal of the day, and surely not the last.

UNDER WATER

In silence, every sound is supposed to speak
like bells under water: gong, monsoon rain,

tiger-striped wind. Every touch,
a quiet breath fanning out into rivers

of your cleansed nerves. Open your eyes,
a fisherman waits, cautiously smoking a cigarette

on the banks of the Ganges. His gray
stubble reminds you of dried, torn sage

on the road to Laramie. Breathe in
the hundreds of miles north

where the Brahmaputra has drowned 200 this week,
where authorities in Assam once again deliver

shoot-at-sight orders amidst renewed ethnic violence
in the Barpeta district. Someone died today

in Banaras from heart failure in the theatre
when they showed newsreels of Gandhi in the 40's

touring cotton mills in Lancashire, England,
making salt at the Bay of Bengal. You watch

a sadhu on the banks, long gray hair matted,
his bony body smeared in sacred ash

from cremation grounds. Recall how Shiva
caught Ganga in his hair when centuries

before it brought in waves to earth heavenly stars
and galactic sense. You breathe in bells

under water, the world bending in willow.
Catch the gong of a grape

calling through a jungle floor, the dark
still of sound in a tiger

lapping last night's storm
from pools in a palm leaf. Listen to the flow

of the river through new openings
in your nerves. Feel dhobis beat strips of clothes

hard against river-rock, against flute holes
in your expanded heart, laying them out

to dry on steep stone steps
like slabs of raw buffalo meat pulled out

of the dark water in 1880's Dakota.
The world is having its way again. Always

the same sound of salt scraping its feet
on shore for apples, same invisible

mosquitoes disturbing your dark
with the flu-like fire of malaria, exact shift

of moths at the window startling
you, as if you are the candle

they seek. Always the pulp in your stomach,
even before your morning juice. 22 Kuki Tribals,

having bathed in the river, are ambushed
on the Imphal-Tamenglong road.

Bones of Mogul horses wash up four centuries
later in the current. The crush of a temple bell drifts

through sunlit waves, cracks like lightning
last night in the lines, sounds like a fish

caught in stiff seaweed hair, working
against the beard of a man

worried about the sudden growth spurt
in the youngest of his family of eight.

It glows with carcinogens, its fibers
containing the power that made the city dark.

III

A Theory of Tongues

INTRORSE

1.

Power in the city again goes
out, but you've always felt comfortable
in the dark, have loved watching a worm

work moonlight into an inward curving
strand, have longed forever for eel-fire inside
the axis of your stance. Even as a child

of six you could enter molecules
of sound in your spine at a moment's
pause, crawl into the storage room

of your grandfather's towel service
on Ewing Avenue, and place Chicago
in the thick blackness of what everyone thought

was an afternoon nap, feeding silence
on a bundle of tablecloths stained with spinach,
stewed lamb, and wine. You could hold a green

oak leaf in your left hand for hours
and hear a gong coming to your groin,
purple forming in your forehead

a lost word, speechless from the flight
and bruised, but humming like a hemichordate
in currents of underwater sound, a takahe

taking hold of wool in air. How many
hours did you lie awake, drinking starlight
through the soft spot in your head, the scent

of a stranger passing through your hips
unnoticed as she adjusts a thin green scarf
in the dark? How many years

did you imagine India inside you, cuddling
afterwards, even sharing a smoke, perhaps,
or a moist pan leaf, only to wake and find

the sheets damp, blue-black ink gathering
at your chest? But no monsoon has come
yet this year to Banaras, no calm

from the 122-degree heat. Air conditioners
stumble, fans slink, and your landlord steals
electricity. Power leaves the entire city

each night, unexpectedly, at precisely
9:13. But you haven't yet eaten dinner and grab
a rickshaw anyway, tunneling through

the chaos of scooters, goats,
and dung. The great swoosh of flies
in tails of water buffalo. The evening

meal beginning its slow revolution
in cauldrons on corners, in woodpiles
near the sawmill on Madanpura. Kerosene

of shopkeepers fluid as spruce, caught
a moment like tropical blood
in a tsetse fly, gasoline in the moon.

2.

You catch yourself
staring at a cripple

on a wooden fruit cart
near Durga Temple,

her left foot
a stump wrapped in

rags, her right arm
turning the wheel

that powers
her cart,

that pulls her
through the darkness

of fifty or sixty
years. Imagine

sharing a mango
with her

leprous mouth, peeling
away layers

of cholera,
which have gathered

piss and shit
all summer in the skin,

one strip
at a

time, holding
that orange

firmness to her
lips, licking

the pulpy juice
as it runs from

the corners
of her mouth.

Moonlight
in the shape

of a palm bends
over you, lightens

her hair a moment
with coconut

fire. Fierce,
the sound

of her milk
enters your

spine. Consider
the comfort

of worms
working themselves

in soil
into something

bent, something
curved. She watches

you watch her,
hand outstretched

as you pass
on a cobblestone street

in the rickshaw-
thick dark. *Baksheesh,*

she moans,
sounding like

a calf, looking
remarkably

like someone's
mother.

3.

Eel-fire in the stance of a palm.
You remember turning inward, hearing
a voice in the lovely darkness

above the crib, in the humming
of galaxies as you sit
in silent meditation. The shells

of coconuts scrape in a mesh bag. A conch
washes ashore onto the beach
of the Arabian Sea. A cottage

in eelgrass, a log turning with
fleas. Unlit lamps unlit. Windows nailed shut
with nails. Layers of sand unfold,

contain sea horses filled with stars
that fell into thin ribs
of sea salt, that could not contain their heat?

Burning with desire to lose desire,
you ask yourself whether you'll ever strike clear
through to sound? Whether a shell

in a bag is really the shell
or the bag, or a tegumentary analysis
in a moment of isolation? Whether a bell

around a cat's neck is a piece
of fruit, or someone's mother
chanting your name over a vista

of birds? Whether it's a mantra
in the bend of grass, or a current
that goes out all over the city, a power

that stirs you from sleep, dampening
sheets? Even as a child
you loved her hair in wind, sought her

on Chicago street corners, in lemon
and tea, in the 1950's blues
of Ray Charles, in orange flower

water, in soiled laundry of the storage
room, in a second helping. Craved her voice
in your chest, a starfish in sand throbbing

for night sky, the ink-blue blood
of a jellyfish. A hemimorphic sound
touches tones with breath lightly

at each of the nerve ganglia
in the spine. *Chakras*, the sadhu
in Banaras explained, grazing your

forehead in monsoon dark
in a grass hut, the call
of your own clarity

of purpose, of complete
attention to the inhalation
of a coconut, the exhalation of a mango,

to a piece of burning
straw. Even as a child
touches a star and holds galaxies

in breathing sea horses, darkness may deepen
to lightning. You listen through
the thunder of a bicycle wheel, through

the cat's eyes of your rickshaw
wallah turning into an alley
of goats, a water buffalo

calf bellowing the dusk in long
even snorts, its moist tongue
pink and reaching a thickness of hope

past the thin beard of the young. To be alive
is to lick the flames of your words, silencing
them with saliva, or to cry out

into the flesh of another?
To face fire as a desire for touch,
or a desire to touch

the inward sounding bells? It calls
across cobblestone for its mother.
Intromittent chords carry through wood smoke,

kerosene, cauldrons of black beans,
which hold the city's power, dark,
but more alive now than before.

IF ON THE TRAIN TO BOMBAY

You will board the train without luggage, with only
a green backpack and a string of rudraksha beads.

You will see silken bees in their throats
as passengers pump their faces like bluegill,

stir from sleep, and begin to wake
with a saw-blade motion. You will ask for a dosa,

a samosa, anything to help you swallow a little more
easily. You will draw train curtains to avoid blood

in your face, to avoid the fate of Kumar Kulkarni,
the actor's son who died last week from stray rocks

from invisible hands of field workers along these same
tracks. You will drink tea. You will drink tea and hear

a hummingbird bring perfect water to your right
nipple, the thrust of tiny wings in your throat.

You will need to urinate, but you will hold it
at first. Then you will really need to urinate,

and you will walk the long aisle back, swaying
from side to side through two cars to the room.

The churning in your groin will be a premonition
of unrequited love. You will not find

a Western toilet but a hole in the floor
with tracks being eaten below it.

You will wonder why the golden arc of your tea
so effortlessly lays itself along the silver threads,

divides in majestic waterfall motion as it drops
a banana peel to a lake floor. You will touch

your silver bracelet and suddenly crave more tea.
You will find your seat after waking from the dream

of the man next to you as he stirs, wet—you think—
from a sudden orgasm brought on from friction

in the last town, from the leopard and the tree.
But your seat will float like a cloud. And what you want,

you will want. Passengers will not see
you climb the secret ladder. They will weep

together all at once for the blood of Kumar
wrapped tightly in a cabbage leaf, left

in a Bombay alley for pigs. They will try
to forget their fear, the smashing of an orange

crayon, theft of a second grade lunch, night walk
in an ink well with nothing but braids. Then they will eat

dosas, or samosas, and drink tea. Then they will need
to urinate and walk the long aisle immediately, swaying

from side to side, grasping seat-backs like moments
of love that they hold an instant and release

as they make their way to the hole. They will return
and, remembering their father's scolding when they

were three, draw the curtains to avoid
invisible hands of field workers, dusty arms

of factory smoke beckoning them outside Bombay.
Your fingertips will throb as they handle the dark

threads. The men will sleep, the women will read
to their sons tales of princes and kings and Mogul

warriors. Mothers will translate the *Mahabharata*
into one of the three lost languages

of salt. And boys will be men who will really
still be boys. Silken bees will feed

the engine, laying tiny drops of perspiration or honey
on windows, steam in the throats of faces

you pass on the tracks. And you will pass feces.
And you will need to cough, though not from the feces

or even from the vacant face near the tracks
of a beggar woman you're certain you loved once

in another life centuries before when you swept floors
together and slept on straw mats and her name was Chitra.

But you will hold it, swallowing hard your memory
of your brother at nine in the hospital with pneumonia,

of your being home alone for the first time
when they all visited him when you were five, the phone

screeching after you from room to room,
the phone screeching. Then you will cough fiercely

as you enter Victoria Terminus. Women will pass
in veils, hunched into their tuberculous pace.

A spot of blood forming on your window. In your
handkerchief. In your Padre Pio palm. Scores of men

will rise from the pavement at precisely 8:58, stretch and
yawn, pick up their mats and walk. They will toss

their newspaper pillows to the tracks that continue
on to Central, to St. John's, to Churchgate, and further

north into Gujarat. The motion of bees
will enter their throats, a hummingbird drawing

perfect water from a tube in the limp they have
temporarily lost. Then they will stumble

from side to side, suddenly remembering their weight,
looking for a place to pee, already wet with a hardness

brought on by intuiting the sexual fantasies of passengers
who boarded in the last town. They will want dosas

or samosas or a cup of tea. They would almost kill
for a biscuit and a little milk. The screech of steam

will be your name, will divide daylight into sundial
fog, will tell you that you have finally arrived.

CYGNUS AND OLOR

Palm leaves outside your Poona hotel room
go dark, bend in a monsoon morning

where just this year 80,000 people
are homeless in Maharashtra alone.

Four weeks of steady rain, you think,
and yet you still thirst. Below

the Deccan Plateau, the syconium of a fig
waits like an abandoned lover. Two men

meet by chance, pass on the street,
and bow deeply at the waist. One says,

Namaste. The other says, *Namaste*.
A child with diarrhea picks her nose and craves

a cup of curd. A young swan in the courtyard
of a prince knows instinctively to extract

only milk from a mixture of water and milk,
but how does one learn to live

in the world and not be touched by it?
You chant *Cygnus* and *Olor* like a secret

mantra, opening the energy center
dormant behind your heart. The exoskeleton

of a roach, you realize, is really softer
than the sconce that dimly lets you see

it. Than the candle wax that drips
to the floor into two watery s-shaped curves.

The sclerite of a mosquito are at once
both smaller and larger than the plates

that shift along the back of a rhinoceros.
You pick up a stick, sclaff the ground

as if tapping for water, step out
onto the verandah to scour constellations

for Cygnus. If you can find it only once,
you wonder, will the cavity in your stomach

finally fill with light? The soft spot
at your skull feather over or become hard

as a wall bracket? Will you travel
from town to town tapping the earth

for starlight with your cane, mumbling *Oh, Olor,*
but where is my Olor? It must be something

in the preparation of food, some spice
that makes spinach in the sag paneer

taste like a palm leaf singed with rain.
You're dizzy with the thought of it, stunned

with months of curry and turmeric bathing
your cells with fire, crying in your gut

for milk, wish you too could bow deeply
like any man or woman who owes a swan.

But how, you wonder, can hot wax pour evenly
into two s-shaped pools? How can the skeleton

of a mosquito outweigh that of a rhinoceros?
There might be a brush fire that some see

as hair. There might be a postage stamp perceived
as a drop of frozen water. There might be

an empty jade box under the cot full of the sound
of bones. The looseness this last month

in your stool is a way of seeing
life from inside a burning star,

water finally forsaking water
in its steady movement toward rain.

ON THE MULA RIVER BRIDGE

Monsoon rains fasten themselves to the groaning
river below like liquid leeches.

And mud from Kashi somehow darkens
the Mula, all the way here in Poona.

On the north bank of the river, among
waving ghostly reeds, a familial rat

keeps drowning. And Ganesha, in sun-stripped
orange, is struggling to raise his trunk.

The houses of the poor splinter with wind.
Their black plastic tarps sag in July rain

like conquered flags, or tongues of those asleep.
Those who die in Kashi, it is written,

go straight to heaven. But the dead in Poona
simply keep dying. *To be a ghost*

in Kashi, the sadhu tells you, *is even*
better than having heaven at all.

At river's edge, a man in orange turban
wades into the fast Mula mud. The hump

in his back is a pond that swells with moonlight,
with a midnight owl loose in his kurta.

A strange mist lifts and unfolds from the trees.
Rain falls to earth like so many dead birds.

USHA VISHNU BHARMAL

1.

The body of a thirteen-year-old girl
is pulled from the Mula River near

Dimbhe Dam. For months, her father imagines
a parrot in his pants, a green tortoise

moving through his sheets, a storm overturning
his launch, pouring his family

into the current. Above him, he sees
the soft belly, water-soaked brown

like a young girl's. He cannot forgive
the meteorologist, drunk on bogwood and paint,

the woman in Mysore who brought her son into her bed
after he had died of the plague, dressed him

in silk kurta and pajama, burning him
a week later in her own grille

when her daughters complained of flies.
He cannot remember his daughter's braid, or

the scent of chestnuts and corn
roasting in monsoon mist on the wooden cart

near the corner before they left, recall
citizens of Poona mourning his loss, pelting

members of the Bombay Engineering Group
with stones pulled from pockets as they

reached to recover the corpse, catching
his daughter, Usha's, wrist.

2.

You wake in the night to find a gold bangle
and a lock of black braided hair on your pillow,

your mosquito net untucked from your bed-
sheet, the window open. A humming

at your ear slowed down
like underwater speech is malaria

that takes a year to arrive. You wonder why
you ever quit smoking, why you traveled

8,000 miles just to sit all day in your hotel
writing in rain. You develop a taste

for chlorine, want to brush your teeth
with vinegar and sea salt. *Usha Vishnu Bharmal,*

you say softly three times, with your head
turned to the left, a fish caught

and tugging on a Bengali sail. *Usha
Vishnu Bharmal,* you repeat once more, tonguing

the bangle like mantra diksha inscribed in the tubes
of your right ear. You wonder why

you quit loving strangers,
never began to, fully, in the first place,

even back home. Why your wife's thin wrist
in the dark reminds you of a rare green

bird. Why you spent so many years
clogging your nerve channels

with booze. Why people barely notice
your limp, even in India,

even when you empty your pockets
and leave the stones on your desk.

3.

A face floats above you, pale-
anemic-tornado-green, dark hair

of a watery reed brushing cheek. The tortoise
shell is an ivory void, brittle darkness turned

inside out, carved with short and broken
lines, an *I Ching* hexagram. *Before Completion,*

you understand in soggy lightning
cracks of sleep, in the way your heart begins

to open, in the pace of your toes finally refusing
the moorings of mosquitoes, in unmouthed vowels

on your desk, the sudden parrot brilliant
in your pie. The kick in your stomach, you realize,

is not a chestnut or an ear
of corn, but a corpse looking to give birth

to starlight, a young girl's laugh
like a galaxy caught on a meteor

reef. You go under water to find her,
hold your breath to the count

of 108, and still don't hear planets
shifting in your spine. You float

through heavens at the bottom
of the Mula and never reach, in tongue,

the syllabic springs of that braid. You consider,
then, inventing a vaccine for bubonic plague,

just to confuse the rats, and yet can't hear
Jupiter gathering in your groin. Contemplate,

that is, placing a corpse in your own bed
just to con mosquitoes, but still never

understand that fierce itching
in the dark. You decide to examine your wrists,

they contain sulfur oxide, faint traces
of purple and green. *Usha Vishnu Bharmal,*

you hear in the bumps on your skin,
through the net, the buzz penetrating

your pillow, entering your limp. *Usha Vishnu Bharmal,*
pours out into reeds, into pocket lint

and pebbles on your desk. Tones in your right ear
raise ancient Brahmanical dust

to bathe mosquitoes with gold, to give
his daughter a home, to dissolve

fist-shaped stones, to finally cup the wrist
of a stranger and call it

your own. *Usha Vishnu Bharmal.*
You tongue monsoon rivers

in her braid, hear her bangles
muffle underwater vowels,

dissolve to pure sound, mouth mantras
into your sheets, into her sleep.

ELUTRIATION

Drink chai steaming with sugar
and milk from a small, narrow glass

on a monsoon afternoon as you leave Poona
Station, easing out of the old iron sheds

toward Bombay. Consider chives back home
in the States lacing boiled red potatoes

with flecks of fluid green light. A Greek diver
on Epiphany in Tarpon Springs, Florida

sinking to sand in search of the silver
cross. When he touches its glint, the point

between your eyebrows, miles away, begins
to throb, and ore from salt-cliffs

settles into your heart, soil from Indiana
washing with the Wabash all the way

into Illinois. The world is having its way
again. Rain settling inside the tunnel you pass

through on the Deccan Plateau is not rain,
simply, but the core of a mountain

elutriating moss into shards
of dark water. You listen through

the historical struggle of border wars. Moguls
in Maharashtra. The Algonquin in Illinois.

The buzz of a silken bee in your throat. Look through
steaming chai, through smoky glass of a train car

into a mountain solid with moss, jungles swaying
with monsoon, with the shrinking territories

of ants in the left eye of a tiger. The Deccan
Express is slow, you think, the mountain

moving in pantomime as you gradually climb
to 5,000 feet. Men and women in fields

below like iron weights sunk to the floor.
Water buffalo in blur pulling the ancient

load. Fields of eelgrass or underwater
reeds. To see rice, finally, as simply

rice might mean that your wife's wrist
in the dark is really, after all, not the leg

of a rare green bird, or even the pace
of a pear tree blossoming milk

in moonlight. To behold eluvium inside
a mountain pass is a way of hearing your own heat

embedded in polar ice. Your definition of distance
cracking like afternoon dashboards of taxis in Bombay

August. Might say more, really, about ossicles
of the blind, or even about the dark space that opens

brilliant a moment when you meditate
perfectly on the slosh of silver tracks

decanted below you as you continue
to climb. And humming are parallel rails

as centuries of sediment or seed. And humming,
the world, again, is having its way,

a tunnel widening into thinning space
in the innermost channel of your spine. You close

your eyes, hold your hands in silent mudra, slip
inside the upward churning vowel, hear wheels

within wheels of the train carrying you
like a world that will not stop.

Like a watery vowel that, bending
in willow, will not ever stop.

SITTING IN THE DARKNESS
WITH BABAJI

An old sadhu steps out of the darkness,
here, at the ashram of the Udasins.

Power is out again throughout Banaras,
but electrical storms not only precede

monsoon, they're in your spine
just with the presence of this 80- or 90-year-

old man. The Yoga shastras are right,
you think. Just the sight of a saint

is enough to change your life, coax
Kundalini to lift its serpent head

a bit. The scooter that brought you
and your guide, Mishra, here is parked

outside ashram grounds, its front wheel turned
toward the darkness of the inner courtyard.

Babaji, Mishra calls, and the old man comes
closer, long gray beard knotted with rubber band,

years of renunciation wrapped in a thick jata
of hair just off his crown. You're introduced,

but the holy man already knows you, he says
with his eyes. How many incarnations you both waited

to enter each other's breath, to heal
one another for an hour, maybe, by chance in dark

temple grounds somewhere on India's
northern plains, a bell ringing the distance

as if from your other body. You sit
like old friends, you three, a few yards

from two water buffalo tending their cud
in the court, and you hold hands, eel-fire

beginning its slow journey upward through oceans
in your spine. Babaji holding Mishra's right hand

with his left, your left hand with his
right. They talk together in Hindi,

but you are not alone. You understand
fully the soft texture of his fingers

gently pressing yours over and over,
rhythmically, as if counting japa

on rudraksha beads. They are thick
not only with years but incarnations

of knowing. An occasional word or phrase
shakes loose from Hindi into your soul, *United States,*

professor, research on sadhus. And the old man
tells you with his hand that he loves you,

but for none of these. *You must learn
Hindi,* he says after many silent moments.

Then you can write for us as well. Mishra's translation
has less force than the yogi's tongue that enters you,

each foreign sound working familiarly with his fingers
further into your hand, up through your heart. You watch

this scene from electric tips of fingers, from steep
temple walls and tops of peepal trees that bend

above this gathering, from tails of water buffalo
gently swaying the darkness down, and wonder

at this sudden dispersal of self, your cells singing
with mantras of the old man's tongue, with the press

of his knowing flesh. You have longed to come
to India for twenty-one years, have met many sadhus

these months, have researched silence
in libraries, ashrams, even in the darkness

of grass huts. But now in holding hands
only briefly with this old man, you feel eels

begin to lift through oceans of planets
in your spine, the world starting

and ending in pulsing light. You remember,
a moment, your other life, those colleagues and relatives

who think Yoga means *new age* or *exotic crystals*
or *weird vegetarian cuisine* or *just another opiate.*

The quiet, generous restraint
of certain friends who struggle

to understand, who have known you
for many years and now believe you

a bit dogmatic but trust in who you are.
But there is no dogma here in your fingertips,

in flight over temple walls, in the brushing
of a buffalo tail against the evening air

you are. In singing cells. They should believe
what they believe. That is all we have.

That is all *anyone* has. For you,
there is no room for doubt

where galaxies dissolve to sound, unwind sudden snakes
in your spine. You feel your life begin

to end, the space of the universe take its place.

PREPARING TO LEAVE

You are preparing to leave this world
of rickshaws, hunger, and sweat. You are

preparing passage through dung-caked walls
hardened by the press of careful hands

and blowtorch sun, by the faraway look
of women and men all day at the chopping block,

cutting stones with picks or gravel
rakes for roads in Varanasi or Calcutta

or Delhi, which are always in need
of repair. You have imagined this moment

for many months, even before you
arrived, the way an avatar might

who descends from some distant star knowing
his or her scars on earth will be brief

and that, when leaving again, new ties will need
to be sliced if one is to throb, perfected, in galaxies

of sound. But you are no avatar nor Buddha-mind,
you know, can hardly lift the lightning

dawn from the dark coal below into your heart,
have too often looked upon malaria and leprosy

and fleas of plague as something separate
from who you are, as something you hope not to become.

The way a child pissing by the water pump
at Bhelupura becomes the dysentery

you're certain you'll contract
in Calcutta. No, this loss won't wash away

the dark fires that have aged
your hands, soot that has gathered

about you for months like patches of rust
that leave holes everyone on the road

can see. This leaving thins out like the last
trace of paint on a wire brush, cuts across rails

that thread through Howrah Station, Victoria
Terminus, and Churchgate, and begins

to narrow over the Arabian Sea
and far past America, out there

where Euclid faltered, and parallel lines
do intersect near some strange

star. You are having your palm read again,
this time by Mishra, as you share tea

together in his flat on Lanka for maybe
the last time. You both know it, can sense the end,

but choose instead to speak of simple things
like cups or biscuits or the reaching of a spoon

across borders of the tablecloth his wife Bina
wove—even their son's name, *Setu,* meaning

bridge. And holding your hands
in his, your palms up like two fleshy planks,

he confirms what everyone else has seen—
that double heart line that makes you fit

for Bhakti, devotion, and embers you have scored
and brought over across dark waters of other

lives. *The search for your Cosmic Beloved
is all that will matter this time,* he confides, *and is all

that you worked so hard for before.* How your struggles
with staying in the world or leaving it

did not begin in 1956. Or even with that spark
of sound your father sent into the moist mouth

of your mother when his body tightened
one night, and he felt further down

cords of starlight knot in his groin
and suddenly loosen as strands of tone

or seed. Her body opening to receive
as her own not only his moaning

but the lull of the liquid vowel
you, still without name, had become.

How centuries before, a stranger with leprosy
might have brushed your sleeve

on a busy street, perhaps in need
of repair, in Varanasi or Calcutta or Delhi,

and you felt her for an instant, fully,
as yourself. Smelled in her blood-blotched cloth

the friction of a thousand burning stars, knowing
there was something more than the skeletal

cages you two had become. Saw yourself fluid
in her pus-filled arm, the cordate

stump. Dissolving in stench
of rotting flesh. Becoming absorbed

in the many ways starlight auscultates
on clear nights, descending, unhindered, to earth

when it lays evenly across damp grass
its varied forms, sounding the planet

with soft impenetrable light
from distant galaxies you can see, can almost

hear—can smell, even, in the spark
of your hands—but cannot yet reach.

A THEORY OF LEPROSY,
A THEORY OF TONGUES

1.

A leper girl leans into your autorickshaw
in Poona, touches your pant leg with curled index finger

wrapped in blood-spotted gauze. She murmurs,
Baba, please. Monsoon rains fasten themselves

like leeches to your sleep, wash everything
away. 80,000 are homeless this year

from floods in Maharashtra alone. In the hotel
you give your pants to the dhobi for washing, immediately

rinse your hands. You imagine blood
on your fingers, blood of *that* finger. The carcass

of a camel is pulled from the trunk
of a Maharaja in Banaras. You carry it home

on the plane, unknowingly, in a green flight
bag, feel an ache in your shoulder,

suddenly develop a thirst for well-water
far back in your throat as you pass through

customs, feel the massive gray sand
of sky-clad tents tilting

to caravan music, of a lone elephant,
shift through your sleep. It stares

at you when you wake in Indiana
in your morning oats, in the evening

mall. In the hysteresis of your job.
The thin scent of an ankle

bracelet pitches through the sulfur
of a six-lane highway during Delhi

rush-hour traffic. Something
in your life, you realize, is

stuck. Something keeps thrashing like a fish
in sand working against the inside of your throat.

2.

Catch a glimpse of gold. A carp washes
ashore, bloated. It carries flecks of sunlight

in its scales, shags them into each receding
wave like something ancient. Pilgrims gulf out

in long herds to the Ganges. You watch
a corpse at the cremation ghat, gold coins

filling his eyes, suddenly changed forever
by the flames. To live honorably

is to die in the heat of one's desires,
or to die *to* desire? His ashes flee

like Brahmanical soot. Like starlight,
your thoughts scatter. The sudden lift of sparrows

is shotgun fire at Godaulia Crossing
four years ago during the Moslem-Hindu

riots. Men from Afghanistan lay down their arms,
then their legs and penises, then their

tongues, one after the other, in a circle
around a pile of burning bones,

in some shamanic rite. Their bodies stiffen
with the rush of blood. They look

like archaic torsos of Greeks. Frozen air
fills your lungs, as bluegill pass through

a gray sponge on the kitchen sink. A sudden shift
of the earth's plates in Hyderabad is not a chance

occurrence, but a longing for connection, energy
trapped in the throat of a hyrax, mass karma

in the root of a hyssop buried
beneath the city. Why else

would it rain so often on a Monday,
even in India, even in the States?

3.

An oriole pours its morning color through Indiana
oak. She reaches for your hand, *I know*

there's such a thing as suffering,
but it doesn't have to be painful. You hear

your wife's words like soft steps of water buffalo
crowding the narrow lanes of Banaras, muffled

in monsoon, like the rut of an autorickshaw
in Poona. Like scales of music

at the back of your throat, a carp
caught in suppressed seaweed breath.

You want to say her name, or even *know* it,
or at least mouth the syllables for, *auburn braid*.

You want to say, *It's good to be home,*
good to have things again like toilet paper

and pizza. Maybe whole-wheat bread would help,
crusty and rough, straight from the toaster.

Maybe you could coax it out with butter,
with silk waves of jazz. You try Sonny Rollins,

but a green parrot perches in the sax, struggles
for supremacy with chunks of gravel, sand shifting

in the belly of the bass. Limbs emerge
from roadside rubble in Hyderabad,

from floods in Poona, a live dog
eating a dead dog near the Banaras cremation ghat.

Part of you is still missing? Part remembers
sea-lice in the dog's ear. You try sarod,

you try coffee, but your nerves tighten
and quake. Consider prying it loose, severing

your frenum with a razor, placing gauze
beneath your tongue. To speak well is to be silent

about it all, or to sing like a tanager,
court the hypoglossal camels? To wake up

trapped in your morning
oats is to die like a hypochondriac

in a vacuum tube? Some electron
is always truant, spinning in the remains

of last night's saliva. Someone always murmurs,
Baba, please, in rustling leaves,

in your wife's fingers. You examine your hands.
Stains ripen like desire, like strawberries

in July, darkening to silence.
To speak of your mistakes would be

in bad taste. To publicly mouth
your failures with a leper girl, a confession,

not a kindness but an act
of colonization? To give her

your tongue, a timocracy? You don't want to live
inside anybody's stain. You don't want the Punjab

in a camel's coals. You simply want
one more night of Poona moonlight,

monsoon grass damp beneath
your feet. The tilt

of her head toward you like a sunflower,
bending in rain, full of fire.

Indian Terms
and
Notes

Indian Terms

Terms are defined at the time of their first appearance and often appear in subsequent poems as well.

The Theory and Function of Mangoes
ghat: steep steps leading down to a river, where pilgrims perform ritual bathing (bathing ghat) or are cremated (cremation ghat). Banaras is well-known for its long string of bathing and cremation ghats that line the west bank of the Ganges River.

Banaras: a former name of Varanasi and the most sacred city in India, commonly considered throughout India as the "oldest continuously inhabited city on earth."

Hysteresis
sadhu: Hindu holy man.

Ganga: the Ganges River.

Mud
tabla: a small drum-like instrument of stitched goatskin, popular throughout India; a pair of kettle drums played with the fingers.

gherao: in India, a coercive tactic adopted during labor disputes whereby workers surround and detain an employer on his own premises until he agrees to their demands.

sitar: a stringed instrument of India, made of seasoned gourds and teak, containing either six or seven playing strings and thirteen sympathetic resonating strings.

Photograph: A History of Maps
rickshaw: a small two-wheeled carriage in which passengers are transported. The old rickshaws, pulled by men, are outlawed throughout India except in Calcutta and in one or two hill stations. Most are now bicycle-powered rickshaws.

wallah: seller of certain goods or provider of services (as in rickshaw wallah).

Poona: a former name of Pune, a city in the Indian state of Maharashtra.

japa: the repetition of a mantra (sacred syllables or sounds, see note under "Colligation at Harishchandra Ghat").

The Fear of Celery
Aghoris and Udasins: two sects, or religious orders, of Hindu sadhus.

Kali: a Hindu deity representing, on a symbolic level, the Void from which the potential, creative force springs. Kali is the "dark" or "black" goddess. Although by some accounts in Hindu literature, Kali represents all three aspects of divine experience—the creative, preservative, and destructive—she is predominantly associated with the "destructive" or "dissolving" force (or Void) that dissolves back into itself all physical manifestations (the creative activity of Shiva) that have issued from it. Kali, as a destructive force or Void, is not considered "evil" (in the Western sense) in Hindu scriptures but contains the creative *potential* of the Void, acting as a complement to Shiva. Thus, although dark and dissolving, Kali simultaneously represents the At-one-ment that is regarded as light and bliss.

Shiva: a Hindu deity representing, on the symbolic level, the "masculine" principle of the universe. Shiva is one of the most important gods of Hindu worship, most often depicted as an ascetic yogi of great self-control. He is occasionally depicted as the husband of Kali, the terrible goddess; when Kali's foot steps on the chest of Shiva's prostrate body, the "creative" activity of the universe dissolves into the Void. Hindu mythology also describes Lord Shiva as "catching" the Ganges River in his hair, cushioning its fall centuries ago as it descended from the heavens to earth (references in "Dawn Boat Ride on the Ganges" and "Under Water" refer to this aspect of Shiva). Banaras is considered "the city of Shiva."

Kali Yuga and Dwapara Yuga: the Hindu scriptures teach that the earth experiences continuous cycles of spiritual evolution and devolution. Each cycle consists of four distinctive phases (yugas) as the earth revolves around the sun, each thousands of years in duration, and each containing more or less potential for spiritual unfoldment, due in large part to the earth's proximity to the sun. Most Indian scriptures teach that civilization is currently near the end of the dark, materialistic age, Kali Yuga. However, the great yogi, Swami Sri Yukteswar, retraced ancient Hindu almanacs and applied their methods of calculation (described by him as more exact and "lost" in the dark age of Kali Yuga). He describes in his 1894 study, *The Holy Science,* that in C.E. 1700 the earth actually entered the next phase, Dwapara Yuga, a more enlightened era when humankind becomes increasingly aware of and able to control "energy."

sushumna: the science of Yoga teaches that in order to attain spiritual unfoldment, a person must learn to penetrate the subtle energy centers in the very narrow "innermost channel" of the spine, the sushumna.

Tantra: a form of Yoga of obscure origin, which emphasizes the awakening of Kundalini (see note under "Sitting in the Darkness with Babaji"), the all-powerful sacred "energy" that lies dormant at the base of the spine.

A Theory of Astronomy as Inscribed in the Book of Blood
Durga: a Hindu deity and form of the Divine Mother in one of Her benevolent aspects.

Vishwanath: an aspect of Shiva as Lord of the Universe; in Banaras, the Golden Temple is dedicated to Vishwanath.

Parvati: a Hindu deity and form of the Divine Mother in one of Her benevolent aspects.

roti: Indian flat whole-wheat bread, most often cooked over an open flame.

paise: a small amount of money, less than a United States penny.

Bone Crushing Bone Is Not an Excuse for Love
Kashi: the scriptural name of the holy city of Banaras.

Colligation at Harishchandra Ghat
pan: betel nut plus chewing additives and various pastes, wrapped in a damp green leaf, and sold in street stalls as a mild stimulant; the chewing of pan often emits a red juice that stains the teeth and corners of the mouth.

mantra: a word or phrase with a particular sound and/or verbal significance. Various mantras, carrying differing psychological and physical effects, are often used in Hindu meditative practices for communing with or attaining to the divine (or unified) experience. They are said to evoke particular states of consciousness and/or material effects.

The Black Bowl
rudraksha beads: strings of Hindu holy beads made from the dried pits of fruit and either worn around the neck or held in the hands to help count the repetitions of mantras or to mark other sacred rituals; ancient rishis (Indian seers) and modern yogis claim that when worn against the skin, rudraksha beads emit helpful electric currents to the body, conducive to good health and deeper meditation.

Dawn Boat Ride on the Ganges
Lord Shiva's hair: see note at the end of Shiva, "The Fear of Celery."

dhobi: one who washes clothes, usually by hand.

Two Plus Two
lassi: a sweet yogurt and iced-water drink common in India.

lama: a Tibetan Buddhist priest or holy man.

Sister and the Boy
sari: a length of lightweight cloth worn as a garment by women.

dhoti: a loincloth worn by men.

danda: a wooden staff or walking stick, emblematic as one symbol of some sadhus' vows of renunciation.

Sahib: a title meaning "lord," often applied to any gentleman and often to Europeans and Americans.

rupee: the main form of currency in India; in 1994 one rupee equaled approximately three United States cents.

Harmonium
harmonium: an organlike keyboard, common in India, that produces tones with free metal reeds actuated by air forced from a bellows.

At Raj Ghat
ji: a suffix often added to names as a sign of endearment and respect (for instance, Gandhiji, Babaji, etc.).

path (pronounced "pot"): road, path.

A Theory of the Borders Between States
Vaishnava: worshipper of God in the form of Vishnu, the "preserver."

Baba: father; a term often given to sadhus as a sign of respect.

Buying Silk
Dasaswamedh Ghat: one of the more important of the ghats that line the Ganges River in Banaras. It takes its name from the belief that Brahma, the Creator, sacrificed (medu) ten (das) horses (aswa) at this site.

Under Water
Shiva's hair: see end of Shiva, "The Fear of Celery."

Introrse
baksheesh: tip; a request for money often used by beggars.

If on the Train to Bombay
dosa: a pancake-like food, often eaten as a snack.

samosa: a deep-fried savory pastry.

Mahabharata: ancient Vedic epics.

Cygnus and Olor
Cygnus and Olor: the genera within which swans are a part. The swan, in yogic scriptures, is considered the mount of Brahma, the Creator. The sacred swan is described as having the power to extract only the milk from a mixture of water and milk; thus, it is considered an important symbol of spiritual discrimination.

Namaste: a Hindu greeting, meaning, "I greet the divinity within you."

curd: yogurt.

sag paneer: an Indian hot dish of cooked spinach and homemade cheese (also often called paneer palak).

On the Mula River Bridge
Ganesha: a Hindu deity, with an elephant head and the body of a boy, who is depicted as riding a rat. He is the son of Parvati and Shiva.

kurta: a shirt, normally blouse-like, with a long square tail to the knees.

Usha Vishnu Bharmal
pajama: pants tied at the waist with a drawstring.

mantra diksha: initiation into the practice of a sacred mantra. The mantra is traditionally given in secret by one's guru into the initiate's right ear at the time of diksha (or initiation into spiritual practices).

Elutriation
chai: Indian tea, made with sugar and milk.

mudra: a sacred hand gesture used in yogic rituals and in the course of performing particular postures (asanas) and meditation.

Sitting in the Darkness with Babaji
Babaji: revered sir; an endearing term often used as a sign of respect for sadhus, particularly those of advanced age (from "Baba," father or sir, plus "ji," a suffix denoting respect).

Kundalini: the all-powerful cosmic energy that, according to yogic teachings, is said to lie dormant at the base of the spine. As such, it is often symbolically depicted as a coiled serpent. In kundalini yoga—an advanced technique that, as yogic and Tantric texts advise, should be undertaken only with the guidance of a realized teacher—the yogi attempts to arouse this all-powerful potential psychic energy in a variety of ways. Upon awakening of the Kundalini energy, the yogi is said to attain cosmic consciousness and, thus, freedom from the duality of multiplicity of conceptual awareness and the constraints of subject/object duality.

jata: thick ropes of the long hair of a renunciant, wound in piles or mounds at the top of the head.

shastras: sacred books or texts.

Preparing to Leave
Varanasi: the presently restored ancient name of Banaras. Varanasi means the city between two rivers (the Varauana and Asi).

avatar: an enlightened being who chooses human incarnation in order to return to earth for the spiritual benefit of humankind.

A Theory of Leprosy, a Theory of Tongues
Hyderabad: a city in south central India that was one of several sites in that area to experience a major earthquake on September 30, 1993. At least 10,000 people perished in this, the deadliest earthquake to hit India since 1935.

sarod: an Indian stringed instrument, resembling a small guitar or mandolin, sounding similar to a sitar.

Notes

The Theory and Function of Mangoes

The phrase, "the knives in the kitchen / drawer with increased affection" is a reference to, and adaptation of, Miguel Hernández's line "looking at knives with affection" from his poem, "I Have Plenty of Heart": Hernández, Miguel. *The Selected Poems of Miguel Hernández and Blas De Otero*. Trans. of poem, Robert Bly. Eds. Timothy Baland and Hardie St. Martin. Boston: Beacon Press, 1970.

The Black Bowl

The quote of Lahiri Mahasaya, *I am drowning in the bodies of many souls off the coast of Japan!*, is from: Paramahansa Yogananda, *Autobiography of a Yogi* (Los Angeles: Self-Realization Fellowship, 1998).

Introrse

The epigraph, *"Who tells me Thou art dark, O my Mother Divine? Thousands of suns and moons from Thy body do shine!,"* is a chant, "Thousands of Suns," from: Paramahansa Yogananda, *Cosmic Chants* (Los Angeles: Self-Realization Fellowship, 1996).

This chant to the Divine Mother refers to Her as dark complexioned, in the form of one of Her sacred manifestations, Kali (see note in Indian Terms, "The Fear of Celery").

I also want to acknowledge the *Indian Express* (Pune, India), whose news stories inspired some of the poems in this book.

Epigraphs and quotations are taken from the following texts:

Vedanta Press, *The Upanishads: Breath of the Eternal*. Translated by Swami Prabhavananda and Frederick Manchester. Copyright © 1948 by the Vedanta Society of Southern California. Hollywood, California.

Federico García Lorca, "Theory and Function of the *Duende*." Translated by J.L. Gili (New York: Grove Press, Inc., 1973).

Paramahansa Yogananda, *Autobiography of a Yogi* (Los Angeles: Self-Realization Fellowship, 1998).

Paramahansa Yogananda, *Cosmic Chants* (Los Angeles: Self-Realization Fellowship, 1996).

George Kalamaras is Associate Professor of English at Indiana University-Purdue University Fort Wayne. He has published two poetry chapbooks, *Heart Without End* and *Beneath the Breath,* as well as poems in numerous journals and anthologies. He is the recipient of a 1993 NEA Fellowship and two writing residencies at the Hambidge Center for the Arts. A long-time practitioner of yogic meditation, he is also the author of a critical study on Hindu mysticism from State University of New York Press, *Reclaiming the Tacit Dimension: Symbolic Form in the Rhetoric of Silence.* During 1994 he spent several months in India on an Indo-U.S. Advanced Research Fellowship from the Fulbright Foundation and the Indo-U.S. Subcommission on Education and Culture. He lives in Fort Wayne, Indiana with his wife, the writer Mary Ann Cain, and their beagle, Barney.